ALICE IN LIMERICK LAND

Alice In Limerick Land

*Whimsical Rhymes from Wonderland
to Delight the Mind and Heart*

by Just Limericks

Table of Contents

INTRODUCTION: WELCOME TO WONDERLAND

Have you ever wondered what it would be like to tumble down a rabbit hole, where the rules of reality are bent, twisted, and turned into something utterly curious?

A world where talking rabbits race against time, a grinning cat disappears into thin air, and a tea party never quite follows the rules?

This book invites you to do just that—take a whimsical leap into the fantastical realm of Wonderland, but with a twist!

Inspired by Lewis Carroll's beloved Alice's Adventures in Wonderland, this collection of limericks brings to life the madcap charm of Wonderland in a fresh and playful way.

From the White Rabbit's hurried dash to the Queen's royal decree, each limerick offers a fun, lighthearted glimpse into the strange and marvelous world that Alice encounters.

The limericks capture the essence of Wonderland's oddities, where sense and nonsense blur together in the most delightful ways.

You'll meet characters that are as familiar as they are strange: the always-late White Rabbit, the mischief-making Cheshire Cat, the cantankerous Queen of Hearts, and the ever-pondering Caterpillar.

With each rhyme, you'll feel yourself sinking deeper into the whimsy, wondering what peculiar twist might be just around the corner.

These poems are more than just playful rhymes—they are tiny portals into a world where the impossible becomes possible and where imagination reigns supreme.

This collection is for readers of all ages, those who grew up with Alice and those who are new to the wonders of Wonderland.

Whether you're here for a quick laugh, a spark of imagination, or a reminder of how wonderful it is to embrace the curious and absurd, these limericks will take you on a delightful journey.

As Alice once said, "I can't go back to yesterday because I was a different person then," and here, in this world of limericks, you too may find yourself transformed by the power of wonder and whimsy.

So, take a deep breath, let your mind wander, and tumble down the rabbit hole once again.

The Wonderland adventure begins now—and who knows where it will lead? With each turn of the page, let the rhymes guide you through the most curious and fantastic world imaginable.

TUMBLING INTO WONDERLAND

There once was a curious lass,
Who followed a rabbit en masse.
Through a hole she did tumble,
With a yell and a grumble,
And found herself on the green grass.

THE WHITE RABBIT'S HURRY

A rabbit with watch in his paw,
Had Alice completely in awe.
"I'm late!" he did shout,
As he scurried about,
Then vanished before she could draw.

The Smile That Floats

There's a smile that floats in the air,
With a mystery beyond compare.
It's wide and it's bright,
A gleam in the night,
A grin that just lingers there.

THE QUEEN AND HER CARDS

The Queen with her cards held so tight,
Commands every game she will fight.
With a flick of her hand,
She will surely demand,
That you play by her rules, or take flight.

A Curious Key and a Tiny Door

A key sat alone on a stand,
Its purpose was perfectly planned.
For a door very small,
That no one could crawl,
But Alice held hope in her hand.

A Flamingo Mallet and Hedgehog Ball

The flamingo mallets were bright,
The hedgehogs rolled with all might,
In croquet they played,
Though the rules were delayed,
The Queen's game was full of delight.

THE MARCH HARE'S WILD DANCE

The March Hare danced in a whirl,
With tea cups and hats in a twirl.
He spun 'round the room,
Making quite a loud boom,
And laughed as the teapot did swirl.

THE QUEEN'S ROYAL DECREE

The Queen, with her temper so bright,
Would scream at the slightest of sights.
"Off with their heads!"
She'd shout in her beds,
And reign with an iron-filled bite.

ALICE TAKES THE STAND

Alice took the stand with great grace,
In the trial, she had to face,
She spoke with such wit,
And never would quit,
Her logic to win the case.

The Cheshire Cat's Smile

The Cheshire Cat grinned wide and sly,
Disappearing as Alice passed by.
He'd wink and he'd nod,
And seem so very odd,
Leaving only his grin in the sky.

The King's Quiet Reign

The King, with his quiet demeanor,
Ruled wisely, but was much leaner,
He rarely would speak,
But his presence unique,
Kept the kingdom in perfect demeanor.

ALICE STANDS TALL

Young Alice, though small, took a stand,
Against madness she'd not understand.
With courage so bright,
She stood in the light,
And made her own fate in this land.

THE GARDEN OF LIVING FLOWERS

In Wonderland's garden, quite rare,
The flowers could talk and declare,
Each with a strange voice,
They'd argue or rejoice,
In a world where the strange filled the air.

THE KNAVE'S STICKY SITUATION

The Knave of Hearts had a plight,
With tarts that had vanished from sight,
He stood in a mess,
With no way to confess,
Caught red-handed, his future not bright.

THE QUEEN'S FURY

The Queen, with her temper so wild,
Would shriek at each thing that beguiled,
Her rage was extreme,
A most fearful scream,
As her fury in Wonderland piled.

THE MOCK TURTLE'S SONG

The Mock Turtle sang songs with great
care,
Of lobsters and dances so rare,
He'd croon with a sigh,
Under the bright sky,
In the Wonderland world, without compare.

A Lesson in Lobster Quadrilles

The lobsters would dance in a line,
With quadrilles that were perfectly fine,
They'd step and they'd twirl,
In an underwater whirl,
All to a rhythm divine.

THE GRYPHON'S GUIDE

The Gryphon would guide through the haze,
With riddles and curious ways,
He'd point with a claw,
At things that left you in awe,
While offering advice in a daze.

THE TRIAL BEGINS

The trial was set with much fuss,
The jury was ready to discuss,
The Knave's fate was grim,
As the courtroom grew dim,
With no one to settle the fuss.

Drink Me, Eat Me

A bottle that said, "Drink Me," stood,
And Alice thought, "Maybe I should!"
She drank and she shrank,
Then later she sank,
In a flood that was not understood.

DRINK ME

Growing Tall and Shrinking Small

One bite of the cake made her grow,
So tall that her head brushed her toe.
Then a sip made her shrink,
In the blink of an eye's wink,
Now where next would her size dare to go?

The Pool of Tears

A puddle grew large from her cries,
A pool formed from watery sighs.
She swam through the tears,
Facing odd sorts of fears,
While creatures around her did rise.

A Race with No Winner

They ran 'round the pool in a dash,
With Alice avoiding a splash.
But when they were done,
No winner had won,
Yet they cheered in a jubilant flash.

Meeting the Dodo

The dodo proclaimed with a cheer,
"We'll race 'til the puddle is clear!"
Round and round they all ran,
With no obvious plan,
And declared, "We've all won it here!"

ADVICE FROM A CATERPILLAR

The caterpillar puffed out some smoke,
And gave advice in a cryptic stroke:
"One side makes you grow,
The other, you'll go
Back to shrinking. Now off!" he bespoke.

THE MUSHROOM'S MAGIC

The mushroom held magical power,
To change one's height by the hour.
A nibble too quick,
Made her grow up thick,
While another made Alice turn sour.

Encounter with the Duchess

The Duchess, so round and so stout,
Had a smile that could cause quite a doubt.
With her baby in tow,
And a temper to show,
She tossed out advice without clout.

THE PEPPERY COOK

The cook stirred the pot with great care,
Adding pepper to fill the cool air.
The kitchen was wild,
With a giggling child,
And a pig who was flying through air!

The Cheshire Cat's Grin

The Cheshire Cat gave a sly grin,
And vanished with just a soft spin.
He'd reappear in a flash,
With a mischievous splash,
Leaving Alice to wonder again.

A Chat with a Puzzling Feline

The Cheshire Cat, wise and aloof,
Spoke in riddles—so strange and so goof.
"You're lost if you stay,
But if you go away,
Which path you take makes no proof!"

The Dormouse's Tale

The Dormouse, with eyes mostly shut,
Told stories while snug in a rut.
He spoke of a dream,
Where things weren't as they seemed,
And Alice just nodded—what a cut!

To the Mad Tea Party!

Alice stumbled into a spree,
Where a hatter was madder than he.
With a hare and a mouse,
They made quite the house,
Of nonsense and sweet tea for free.

TEA

THE HATTER'S RIDDLE

The Hatter posed riddles galore,
That baffled poor Alice to the core.
"Why is a raven like a writing desk?"
She answered, feeling perplexed,
But he only said, "That's a bore!"

THE MARCH HARE'S MESS

The March Hare sat down with a thud,
He spilled all his tea in the mud.
"Quite mad," Alice thought,
"Not a moment was caught,
For the mess was just part of the flood."

PAINTING THE ROSES RED

The gardeners painted with haste,
To turn roses to red with no waste.
They feared for their heads,
As the Queen's temper spread,
And their work was all done in great haste.

THE MOCK TURTLE'S TEARS

There once was a turtle, quite sad,
Whose tears were both endless and bad.
She cried and she sobbed,
While the Gryphon just probed,
Till she laughed and felt not so mad.

OFF WITH HER HEAD!

The Queen of Hearts yelled in dread,
"Off with her head!" she had said.
With a glare and a shout,
She'd cast all doubt out,
But it was only a dream in her head.

THE WONDERLAND DREAM ENDS

The dream came to end, a soft sigh,
As Alice awoke with a cry.
But though it was through,
She knew it was true,
That Wonderland lived in her eye.

THE QUEEN'S CROQUET MATCH

The Queen took her croquet mallet,
While the flamingo made quite the pallet.
With hedgehogs as balls,
And soldiers as walls,
The game was a strange kind of ballet.

The Evidence of Tarts

The tarts, they were stolen, no doubt,
But who took them, they couldn't figure out.
The Knave took the fall,
While the Queen gave a call,
"Off with his head!"—with a shout.

THE QUEEN LOSES HER COOL

The Queen, with a temper so fierce,
Could make anyone's nerves start to pierce.
She shouted and screamed,
Until Alice dreamed,
Of a world where her orders would cease.

AWAKENING FROM THE DREAM

Alice woke with a start, and she said,
"Was it all just a dream in my head?"
With a blink and a sigh,
She wondered just why,
Her adventure felt more like a thread.

THROUGH THE LOOKING GLASS

Beyond the glass, Alice gazed,
At a world where all things were crazed.
Reflections were strange,
And thoughts seemed to change,
In a realm that left her amazed.

WONDERLAND LOGIC, OR LACK THEREOF

In Wonderland, logic's askew,
Where rules simply vanish from view.
A hatter, a hare,
Were perfectly fair,
But the rules? Well, they didn't quite stick
too!

A World of Curiouser and Curiouser

Alice wandered, and found to her glee,
That everything odd as could be.
With creatures so wild,
And a world so beguiled,
She thought, "This is my world, it's for me!"

THE RULE OF THE QUEEN

The Queen was the ruler supreme,
With a temper that was quite extreme.
Her rule was quite clear,
"Off with your ear,
And make sure to do it, no scheme!"

THE RABBIT'S WATCHFUL WORRY

The White Rabbit, so fidgety and fast,
Checked his watch and thought, "I'm
aghast!"
"I'm late!" he would say,
And hurry away,
With Alice now following at last.

A Drink to Change It All

A sip of the potion she drank,
Made Alice begin to rethink.
She grew tall once more,
And then shrank to the floor,
While the drink still remained at the brink.

THE CATERPILLAR'S QUESTIONS

The Caterpillar puffed on his hookah,
And asked Alice questions that shook her.
"Who are you?" he said,
"Not a bit, I feel dread!"
Alice sighed and said, "I'm a looker!"

CONCLUSION: THE END—OR IS IT?

And so, our journey through Wonderland comes to a close, but as Alice discovered, the adventure is never truly over in a world where logic takes a backseat and the impossible is just another delightful turn of the page.

From the bustling haste of the White Rabbit to the unpredictable antics of the Queen, the adventures we've had in this curious land are as fleeting as a Cheshire Cat's smile, but no less memorable.

These limericks, with their playful rhythms and absurd charm, have offered a glimpse into a world where time runs mad, riddles rule, and the strange becomes the everyday.

Perhaps, after reading them, you've found yourself laughing at the whimsy, scratching your head at the logic (or lack thereof), or even feeling a little more curious about the wonders of the world around you.

After all, as Alice herself would say, "I'm not strange, weird, off, nor crazy, my reality is just different from yours."

But just because we've reached the last limerick doesn't mean Wonderland has disappeared—it's always there, ready to surprise you once more.

The key to this world is simple: keep your mind open to the impossible, your heart ready for the unexpected, and your curiosity ever-thirsty for more. Wonderland, in all its madcap glory, is just a thought away.

So, as we leave behind the strange creatures and curious happenings, remember: in the heart of every Wonderland, there's always room for one more twist, one more surprise, and one more delightful tumble down the rabbit hole.

Until next time—if you ever find yourself tumbling again, just follow the smile of the Cheshire Cat. It might lead you right back to the beginning.